BORGLUM'S
M O U N T A I N

A Pictorial History of the Mount Rushmore Memorial • by Stan Cohen

D1307957

BORGLUM'S MOUNTAIN

M O U N T A I N

A Pictorial History of the Mount Rushmore Memorial • by Stan Cohen

Dakota Resources, Inc.
Rapid City, South Dakota

COPYRIGHT © 1983 STAN COHEN
All rights reserved. No part of this book
may be used or reproduced without written
permission of the publisher.

LIBRARY OF CONGRESS
CATALOG CARD NUMBER 83-61083

ISBN 0-933126-34-4

First Printing   May 1983
Second Printing   April 1984

Typography by Arrow Graphics
Cover Art Work by Joe Boddy, Missoula, Montana

BACK COVER:
Sculptor Gutzon Borglum raised the American flag on Mount Rushmore at the mountain's dedication, October 1, 1925. Band music, salutes fired by army troops and flowing speeches by area dignitaries climaxed by a colorful flag-raising ceremony proved to be good publicity for the memorial, but little else. No definite plans had as yet been formulated for construction of the memorial, nor was there money available to begin the project. Work did not begin on the memorial until almost two years later.

Printed in the United States of America
by Walsworth Publishing Company
Marceline, Missouri

DAKOTA RESOURCES, INC.
Box 886
Rapid City, South Dakota 57709

Contents

"The union of these four presidents carved on the face of the everlasting hills of South Dakota will constitute a distinctly national monument. It will be decidedly American in its conception, in its magnitude, in its meaning, and altogether worthy of our country."

—*Calvin Coolidge*

Introduction

Carved into the face of a remote granite mountain, one man's tribute to America brings travelers from all over the world to the Black Hills of South Dakota. They come to see one of the world's greatest man-made achievements, sculpted by Gutzon Borglum, who dedicated 16 years of his life to the project. Doggedly, Borglum pursued his vision through the Great Depression, when money problems repeatedly threatened his grand design. Today, Mount Rushmore is one of the most popular and well-known tourist attractions in the United States, drawing over two million visitors a year. Standing on the veranda of the Park Service Visitor Center, one cannot help but wonder at the awesome and meticulous work that went into this monumental mountain sculpture.

Few realize, however, the extraordinary technical problems challenging the completion of this massive project, or the political battles and financial troubles that beset its artist over a decade and a half as he struggled to create this spectacular landscape of American presidents.

An artistic genius with an unyielding personality, Borglum himself agitated the situation by clashing with others involved in the project and by his clumsy handling of money. He gave a good part of his later life to the mountain, persisting where others would have given up in disgust. In fact, after his death, work stopped in 1941 and the memorial has never been officially declared finished.

I feel the Mount Rushmore story can best be told through the use of photographs, so I have brought together a collection to depict the history of the mountain from 1923, when the project was conceived, to the end of construction in 1941. This narrative does not attempt to examine the many problems of creating Mount Rushmore in detail, but rather provides an historic overview to accompany the photographs, many of which have never before been published. For the best detailed study of the entire construction, including the financial and political history, one should read Gilbert Fite's book, *Mount Rushmore*, first published in 1952.

The mountain stands today as a great memorial to the American people and to the one man most responsible for its creation—Gutzon Borglum.

I wish to thank the staff of the National Park Service, Mount Rushmore National Memorial, and especially Tom Haraden, Park Technician for the National Park Service, for their help and guidance with this project. All the photographs were obtained from the National Park Service, most of them courtesy of Lincoln Borglum. Joe Boddy of Missoula, Montana, painted the cover picture and Arrow Graphics of Missoula typeset the book. Connie Poten, also of Missoula, edited the manuscript.

CHAPTER ONE
Gutzon Borglum

The man who carved Mount Rushmore was born in the rugged wilderness of southern Idaho in 1867, only four years after it was declared a territory. His father, a scholar and medical student, had left his native Denmark in 1864 to seek his fortune in the American West.

Shortly after John Gutzon de la Mothe Borglum was born, the family moved south to Ogden, Utah. A brother, Solon, who was to become a well-known sculptor in his own right, was born there in 1868, and three more brothers and a sister followed. The elder Borglum, making a meager living treating the sick, decided to finish his medical degree in St. Louis. From there he moved his family to Fremont, Nebraska, where he purchased a ranch and set up a medical practice.

Growing up on the frontier, the young Borglum was drawn to the history and lore of the West. He discovered his talent for drawing and painting in grade school and nurtured it through high school, a private boarding school in Kansas. After graduating, he was forced to begin an apprenticeship in a machine shop—making a living as an artist was unheard of in those days.

But Borglum could not abandon his creative urge, so he finally decided to travel to California to seek his fortune in the arts. His father, disillusioned with practicing medicine in Nebraska, followed, moving the whole family to Los Angeles. After two years, the elder Borglum returned to Nebraska, but Gutzon stayed on, rented a studio and hung out his shingle as an artist and art instructor. He associated himself with the noted artists of the area and grew more confident in his ability.

One day in an art class, he met Mrs. Elizabeth (Lisa) Putnam, a widow in her late thirties. A friendship turned to courtship for the 23-year-old Borglum who married Lisa in 1890. At the urging of a new friend, Mrs. John C. Fremont, wife of the famed soldier and explorer, the couple journeyed to Paris, France, to study art. Borglum studied at the Julien Academy and was accepted into the famous Ecole des Beaux-Arts. The renowned French sculptor, Auguste Rodin, influenced Borglum's decision to turn to sculpture over canvas art—and the challenging artistic medium was to consume his life for the next fifty years.

Returning to California in 1891, the couple moved to the little town of Sierra Madre. Soon Borglum's brother, Solon, also ventured West to study and teach art in Santa Ana, California. Ever restless, Borglum decided to move to England. Lisa was tired of moving, and their relationship began to break down. She eventually went back to California alone. The marriage

Gutzon Borglum, sculptor of Mount Rushmore National Memorial, formal portrait (photo 1934). John Gutzon de la Mothe Borglum was born March 25, 1867 in Bear Lake, Idaho to Danish emigrant parents. A man of unusual energy and vigor, Borglum began work on Mount Rushmore in 1927 at 60 years of age. He died on March 6, 1941 as the memorial was nearing completion.

was never to be the same.

Borglum's life was consumed by his art; but personal problems and indebtedness would plague him until his death in 1941. He was never able to manage money to his own benefit.

One of Borglum's best known sculptures is the North Carolina monument commemorating the Civil War at the Gettysburg National Military Park. It was completed in 1929.

In 1902, he moved back to the United States and opened a studio in New York City. He won a gold medal for his statue, "Mares of Diomedes" at the 1904 St. Louis World's Fair. Gaining a widespread reputation for his masterful work, Borglum was awarded commissions for statues and sculptures around the country. Several of his pieces were placed in the rotunda of the United States Capitol.

In 1907 his wife Lisa agreed to a divorce, a great relief to Borglum. The stocky, intense artist moved more freely, becoming friends with prominent figures on the American scene, including President Theodore Roosevelt. Fascinated by the new science of flying, Borglum witnessed one of Orville Wright's flights for the Army in 1908. Another turn in his life was marriage to Miss Mary (Peggy) Montgomery in 1909, whom he had met a few years before. She was a well-educated linguist who had previously helped Borglum with some secretarial work.

The new couple settled in the East and bought a piece of land with several old houses on the banks of the Rippowan River near Stamford, Connecticut. The estate was named "Borgland" and much of Borglum's work was done here in his newly built studio.

The couple's son, James Lincoln, named for Borglum's father and his favorite American, was born in 1912. A daughter, Mary Ellis, was to follow in 1916, named for Mary Borglum and Dr. James Ellis who brought her into the world.

A goal left unfinished was Borglum's plan to fill the Hall of Records with sculptures of many public figures. Toward this end he shapes a clay sculpture of South Dakota Senator Peter Norbeck, one of the founding fathers of Mount Rushmore. A bronze of this work stands in Borglum's studio at Mount Rushmore.

Three principals of the Mount Rushmore project pose for their portrait in 1925. Theodore Shoemaker, left, a South Dakota state forester, located the mountain for Borglum. Sculptor Gutzon Borglum sits next to his son, Lincoln, who spent many years working with his father and would work on the memorial after his father's death in 1941.

Also in 1916, Borglum took on his biggest assignment to date, carving a memorial to the Confederacy on Stone Mountain, near Atlanta, Georgia. Here he met Major Jesse Tucker who would become an invaluable assistant at Stone Mountain and later on Mount Rushmore.

A new dimension to Borglum's career began with America's entry into World War I in 1917. President Wilson asked Borglum to study the problems in the new aircraft industry. Borglum found the industry riddled with corruption and waste, and when the government responded indifferently to his claims he exposed his report to the news media. Involved in national and international politics for years, Borglum met many of the outstanding leaders of the Great War. During the war "Borgland" became a meeting place for the followers of Tomas Masaryk, who was trying to form the independent country of Czechoslovakia in central Europe.

His political involvement fueled his artistic career, and in the years between the end of the war and the beginning of the Mount Rushmore project Borglum became one of the best known sculptors in America, his work in constant demand. His statues were displayed across the nation and he even had a hand in the upgrading of the torch on the Statue of Liberty. In the 1920s he moved his family to San Antonio, Texas, and after taking the commission at Mount Rushmore, bought a ranch near the Black Hills.

Borglum was now ready to embark on his greatest sculpturing contribution to the American people—Mount Rushmore.

Gutzon Borglum

CHAPTER TWO
Conception &
Dedication

The novel idea for a significant rock carving in the Black Hills was the inspiration of Doane Robinson, Secretary the South Dakota Historical Society and a well-known citizen in the state. He approached the state's first citizen, Senator Peter Norbeck, creator of the Custer State Park and an avid endorser of South Dakota parkland and recreation facilities, for support of his landmark project.

Robinson proposed that "a carving or a series of carvings of some of the famous pioneers of the West would be a great monument to America's past and a large tourist attraction for the state." He also proposed that the prominent granitic "needles" in the Hills be considered for the project.

In 1924 this proposal was put forth to the citizens of South Dakota and it elicited strong opposition. Protestors claimed that these carvings would disfigure the natural wonders of the Hills, whose beauty was enough in itself to attract visitors. But Robinson was not one to give up easily; he wanted to put his state on the map. He invited the famous sculptor, Gutzon Borglum, then working at Stone Mountain, Georgia, to come to the Hills and investigate the project.

Robinson led Borglum, his 12-year-old son, Lincoln, Major Jesse Tucker and several dignitaries from Rapid City on a trek over the area in September 1924. The party even climbed the 7,242-foot Harney Peak. Borglum came away from the trip very enthusiastic about the proposal and promised to come back and study the area in more detail. However, he stressed, he was only interested in carving figures of national importance, such as Washington and Lincoln.

Eventually the "needles" site was abandoned as impractical. But a new idea was proposed: to carve the figures on a mountain face large enough to include a giant entablature which would depict nine great events in American history.

When Borglum returned to the area in August 1925, he was searching for just such a mountain to begin his carving. Theodore Shoemaker, the state forester and a man who knew every inch of the Black Hills, was engaged to guide the famous sculptor in his quest for a mountain. Shoemaker took Borglum to a remote part of the Hills northeast of Harney Peak, three miles from the mining town of Keystone. There, a mountain 6,000 feet above sea level loomed over the dark pine forest. It was 1,000 feet long and 400 feet wide. Best of all, it presented a 300-foot perpendicular slab on its east side. It was named Mount Rushmore after a young New York lawyer who earlier had been checking mining claims in the area.

One of the oldest granitic outcroppings in the world, Mount Rushmore is finer-grained and more evenly textured with fewer pegmatitic veins than other exposed mountain roots of the Harney Range in the Black Hills. Thus, it would lend itself to the proposed gigantic carving. It was here that Borglum would begin the colossal achievement of his life. He would struggle with the project until his death at age 74.

An intrepid New York lawyer, Charles Rushmore trekked over the Black Hills inspecting mining claims. Mount Rushmore was named for him.

DEDICATION

A master at showmanship, Borglum was constantly promoting himself and the mountain project across the country. His theory: the more publicity he and the mountain received, the more money would flow into the coffers to keep the project moving. But lack of funds hampered the project for its entire 16-year history; only six of those years were spent in actual work.

It all began on October 1, 1925, when more than 3,000 people trudged up to the base of Mount Rushmore from the tiny mining town of Keystone, three miles away. The crowd hiked on primitive roads and trails to watch Borglum place a flag at the top of the mountain and promise that a completed head of a president could be viewed there in one year.

THE BLACK HILLS

The Black Hills are a range of low mountains in southwestern South Dakota and eastern Wyoming. They cover an area of 6,000 square miles and rise 2,000 to 4,000 feet above the high plains that surrounded them.

Billions of years ago during the Archean period, the hills were formed when pressure from below raised the crust of the earth into a 50-mile-wide dome. Erosion eventually stripped the dome to its granitic core, exposing the gigantic rock outcrops that are the mountains today. Named after General William S. Harney, who led a campaign against the Plains Indians, Harney Peak in the Black Hills at 7,242 feet, is the highest point in South Dakota.

The Sioux Indians, who consider these mountains sacred and once held them as a reservation, named this region the Black Hills because the dense pine forests covering their slopes made them appear black from the plains.

Thousands of miners and settlers swarmed into the Hills when gold was discovered in 1874. Two years later the government forcibly took over the ore-rich reservation from the Indians, and dozens of rowdy mining towns sprang up to serve the gold, silver, copper, lead and iron mines. The most famous of these towns was Deadwood, where Calamity Jane lies buried next to her true love, Wild Bill Hickok.

Today the Black Hills are a world-famous tourist attraction that includes Mount Rushmore, Wind Cave National Park, Custer State Park, ghost towns and the largest gold mine in the United States—the Homestake.

Borglum drew these figures after his first visit to the Black Hills, when the site for the carving was to be the "Needles," a group of granitic spires five miles southwest of Mount Rushmore. The site was abandoned in favor of the present location.

In 1925, before carving began, millions of years of erosion had accentuated the fracture patterns on the face of Mount Rushmore. On his second trip to the Black Hills, Borglum inspected a number of sites, but finally decided on this one. Its southeast exposure appealed to the sculptor because the lighting would enhance the details of his work and add to its aesthetic appeal.

STONE MOUNTAIN

Gutzon Borglum had dreamed of sculpting a massive monument to the American people for many years. He got his chance in 1916, when he was commissioned to carve a memorial to the Confederate soldier on Stone Mountain, Georgia, a crescent-shaped granite mountain 900 feet high and 3,000 feet long. Stone Mountain rises boldly out of the level southern piedmont 16 miles north of Atlanta. The commission would be Borglum's greatest sculpturing challenge to date.

Generals Robert E. Lee and Stonewall Jackson were to be carved in relief with Jefferson Davis, president of the Confederacy. The three leaders would be trailed by a 1,500-foot-long carving that was to portray the soldiers of the Confederacy. Borglum built models, surveyed the mountain and spoke throughout the South to raise money for the project. At the end of World War I he actually began the carvings and worked out the mechanical problems—no small feat since there was no precedent to follow for this vast a project. He would carve the mountain by using dynamite to eliminate the tons of unwanted rock. Work progressed until 1925 when differences between Borglum and the Stone Mountain Monument Association boiled over and he was dismissed.

Although he was never to work on this carving again, the experience on the mountain would prove invaluable to him on his next and last mountainous venture—Mount Rushmore. Unfortunately, problems with the backers of the Mount Rushmore project would also plague him for the rest of his career.

This early model shows only three figures. As the sculptor's plan evolved to include a fourth president, Theodore Roosevelt was added to the group.

CHAPTER THREE
Early Years

With the site chosen and Borglum commissioned, the delicate task at hand was choosing the subjects for the gigantic sculptural endeavor. Borglum had agreed to the project only if the figures carved were national leaders, reinforcing the general consensus that only prominent historical American figures were appropriate for a site of national importance.

Only three figures were originally considered for the monument— George Washington, father of the country; Abraham Lincoln, the man who held the country together; and Thomas Jefferson, author of the Declaration of Independence and leader of westward expansion. Closer inspection of the mountain's face revealed that four figures could actually be carved into the granite outcrop. The suggestion of Theodore Roosevelt sparked off a controversy.

One faction felt that the former president, who had died only a few years earlier, had not yet withstood the test of time to ensure his great leadership qualities. But Borglum, who had been a personal friend and admirer of Roosevelt, spoke out in support of Roosevelt's enduring stature as an outstanding national figure. President Calvin Coolidge, vacationing in nearby Custer State Park, endorsed the choice of Roosevelt, the heroic leader of the Rough Riders in the Spanish-American war, the builder of the Panama Canal, and the frank admirer of the American West who stamped an everlasting influence on the spirit of the nation.

Coolidge's support of Roosevelt for the fourth figure in the monument decided the choice, and his interest in the project brought forth much-needed national publicity, helping obtain the funds necessary to get the project under way.

In the early design stages, Borglum planned to inscribe a 500-word history of the United States, to be written by President Coolidge, on the present site of Lincoln's head. The entablature was to be shaped in an outline of the Louisiana Purchase, 80 feet by 120 feet. But problems arose: there wasn't enough room on the rock face for the essay if the words were to be large enough to read from afar; then Borglum realized that the Jefferson figure had to be moved to the right of Washington, forcing the Lincoln figure to be placed where the essay was planned; and finally, Coolidge backed out of the project altogether, objecting to Borglum's insistence on editing his inscription.

In 1925 Doane Robinson, secretary of the South Dakota Historical Society, set up the Mount Harney Association through the South Dakota state legislature to oversee the project and raise money for construction.

The national publicity brought in an initial $54,000. These funds went fast, however, and President Coolidge urged the state to explore possible funding through the federal coffers.

A ceremonial drilling took place on August 10, 1927, to initiate construction, with President Coolidge in attendance. Borglum and his friend and co-worker, Major Jesse Tucker, had both worked with the Du Pont Company on developing the use of dynamite to blast away rock at Stone Mountain. Their experience in Georgia had prepared them for the engineering problems that Mount Rushmore posed. Tucker was named the director of operations on Rushmore. Most of the mountain would be carved away by dynamite blasting; only the finish work would be sculpted by hand.

The federal government did not take an active role in the project until February 1929, when Public Law 805 was passed, creating the Mount Rushmore Memorial Commission. Rapid City businessman John Boland chaired the committee of 12, and Congress authorized $250,000 on a matching fund basis, providing the real stimulus for construction. Most of the appointees to the Commission were influential citizens who, it was hoped, gave an aura of credibility to the project. Members included the well-known South Dakota judge, William Williamson, an original proponent of the project. Doane Robinson was later appointed to the Commission.

By the fall of 1929 the outline of Washington's head began to take shape, but Borglum suffered a setback when a salary hassle forced his good friend, Jesse Tucker, to resign as mountain construction superintendent. Borglum would now have to spend his days on the mountain himself, supervising con-

A wooden bridge spans a small "valley" behind the heads.

The stairway angles up the crevice of the mountain to a cliffhanging shed.

Workers climbed to their jobs on the mountaintop by these stairs until the tramway was improved enough for their use in the late 1930s.

struction. He had originally intended to simply oversee the overall project and control the artistic parameters of the figures; this would have allowed enough free time for him to work on the other commissions for sculptures that were constantly pouring in.

Almost five years after the first dedication of the mountain in 1925, the figure of Washington was unveiled on July 4, 1930. More than 2,500 people traveled the newly constructed automobile road to see a huge flag raised to reveal the outline of the Nation's first President.

In spite of all the national recognition received by the emerging monument the deepening Depression cut into federal monies needed to keep the men working steadily on the mountain.

Borglum perservered, and in the spring of 1931, drillers were put to work on Jefferson, to the west of the Washington figure. But an able assistant named Hugo Villa seriously damaged the Jefferson site—he had over-calculated the amount of dynamite needed for blasting out the outline. Borglum fired Villa and replaced him with his own son, 19-year-old Lincoln. But the damage proved irreparable and by the summer of 1934 Borglum had reluctantly decided to place Jefferson on the opposite side of Washington. The first Jefferson head was blasted off the mountain.

The Mount Rushmore National Memorial Commission poses in front of the raw face of the mountain in July 1929.

Gutzon Borglum, arms crossed, listens intently to President Calvin Coolidge giving his opening address to initiate construction of Mount Rushmore on August 10, 1927. Following the address, President Coolidge handed Gutzon Borglum a set of drills. The sculptor then quickly ascended the mountain and began drilling the master points for the George Washington figure, marking the official beginning of work on the world's most colossal sculpture.

Lincoln's head did not begin to emerge from the granite core until four years after worked started in 1931. By the mid-thirties, the mountain was coming to life—Washington, Jefferson and Lincoln were well-defined—even recognizable—and preliminary work had begun on Roosevelt.

A shortage of money constantly tormented Borglum and the Memorial Commission. The sculptor took his show on the road for a nationwide fund-raising tour. Months of good working weather passed over idle tools due to lack of financing. Constantly bombarded with requests for money, Congress in 1933 turned the Mount Rushmore project over to the National Park Service, a move that would cause Borglum even more problems in the years ahead.

But progress slowly continued, and on August 30, 1936, President Franklin D. Roosevelt was on hand for the unveiling of Jefferson. Borglum had worked on his national dream through the terms of three presidents and into the Great Depression. There would be many more years of labor ahead, but the memorial was now truly a national monument of major proportions. Doane Robinson's goal of putting South Dakota on the map had come true.

At the dedication in 1936, the handsome and proud Borglum turned to President Roosevelt and said, "I want you, Mr. President, to dedicate this memorial as a Shrine to Democracy."

Work began in 1927; by the fall of 1929 the face of Washington began to take shape.

Although far from complete, the head of Washington was unveiled at a ceremony on July 4, 1930, several years later than Borglum originally promised.

Visitors gaze at the head of Washington from the patio of Borglum's studio in 1934. Jefferson's head had not yet been started.

The face of Jefferson was actually blocked out to the left of Washington, but flaws were discovered in the rock and it was removed in the summer of 1934.

ELEVATION
ONE MILE ABOVE
SEA LEVEL

VIEW
MONUMENT
FROM STUDIO
300 FEET
GOOD TRAIL
INFORMATION & SOUVENIRS

CHAPTER FOUR
Construction Methods

Nothing in modern history approaches the scale of Mount Rushmore. With no blueprints to follow, no precedent to guide him, Borglum took on the challenge of engineering the massive mountain sculpture in tribute to America. He brought together through the years four uniquely capable men to help him execute his grand design: Maj. Jesse Tucker; Hugh Villa; William S. Tallman; and his own son, Lincoln.

Under their supervision, more than 360 men carved away at the granite mountain over its 14-year construction history. Mostly hard rock miners, loggers and ranchers from the region, the men received training by Borglum himself before they set to work, scaling the mountain. The pay scale ranged from 50 cents to $1.50 per hour—depending on the job skill—and no one was killed or even seriously injured on the job. Considering the risks of hanging off the side of a mountain and of working with dynamite and drills, such a success record serves as a special credit to the sculptor's planning methods and to the safety standards imposed.

Borglum first sculpted and cast a small model of the proposed figures at his studio in San Antonio, Texas. He then built a much larger model of three figures in South Dakota, which he installed in his log studio at the base of the mountain. But the mountain would dictate the final art: as Borglum studied Rushmore's fracture patterns and structural integrity he changed the model many times to conform with the massive granite face. The models were scaled so that one inch equaled one foot when transferred to the mountain itself.

Each day, workers climbed a series of wooden staircases—totaling 760 steps—that angled up the steep crevices in the side of the mountain. At the base of the mountain an improbable little worktown was built, consisting of a blacksmith shop, tram shed, tool sheds, and buildings to house the air compressors that provided air for the drills. On top of the mountain, the workers had to build tool and repair sheds, shelters, a small studio and houses for the winches that would lower men over the ledges—all before any work on the actual sculpture could begin.

In 1936 a tram was strung by cable from the base to the top for hoisting tools in a large metal bucket. Later, the tram was strengthened and a wooden box hooked up to carry workers up to work, saving much time and energy.

Dynamite explosions echoed through the Black Hills for years; by the end of construction in 1941, almost a half-million tons of rock had been blasted or chiseled off the mountain. The workers eventually became so expert at precision dynamiting that they could blow away the outline of a figure to within several inches of the surface to be finished. In training the workers, Borglum and his first assistant, Jesse Tucker, drew on their experience with dynamite at Stone Mountain, Georgia. Tons of Rushmore granite had to be removed before a figure would emerge: Washington's chin is 30 feet behind the original mountain surface; parts of Jefferson's and Lincoln's heads are back 80 feet; and Roosevelt's head finally took shape 120 feet behind the original surface.

Drillers sat in leather bosun's chairs or stood on cages that were suspended by cables from the top of the mountain. They drilled a series of holes in various depths into the granite, using pneumatic drills suspended by chains from the crown of the mountain. The air for the drills—or jackhammers—was pumped up a pipeline from the air compressors housed at the base. The blacksmith sharpened several hundred four-star drill bits daily to keep the crews supplied.

The first holes drilled were six to eight feet deep, 15 to 18 inches apart, in a string of 15 to 20 holes. Then powder, stored in magazines on the mountain, was packed into the holes. The crews usually detonated the dynamite at noon and at the end of the working day. As more and more rock was removed, and the drillers approached the final working surface, they drilled shallower holes closer together, using less powder for blasting.

Discoveries of cracks and flaws in the mountain face as the outer stone was removed forced Borglum to make nine major changes in this plaster model. Each modeled head was shifted many times to conform with changes in position of the sculptured figures.

Borglum rides the aerial tram to the top, where work on the presidential heads continues slowly. Installed in the later years of construction, the tram hauled tools, equipment and men to the top.

An unidentified visitor stands on the deck of the hoist house at the base operations. The metal tool bucket was later replaced with a large wooden box that workers could ride in, saving them from the grueling uphill walk to the carvings.

The base camp facilities housed the compressor house, left foreground, the blacksmith shop, right foreground, and the hoist house for the tram, center. The first studio is out of the picture to the right. This 1936 photo was taken from a descending tram car.

Spidery walkways connect the storage sheds and winch houses that crown the top of Mount Rushmore. A steep wooden staircase built up a fissure in the side of the mountain was the only access to the top until the tram car could be installed in the late 1930s.

Other men, known as "pointers," had the most critical job on the mountain. They determined where to drill the holes for the dynamite by using a "pointing machine," designed solely for the sculpture. This unique measuring device, placed at the top center of each proposed figure, was an upright shaft with a 30-foot horizontal steel boom attached to a base plate. The base plate was marked off in degrees of a circle. The boom protruded over the edge of the mountain, suspended from the shaft by thin piano wire. The entire "pointing machine" was anchored by cables bolted into the granite. This way, it could swing in an arc to make measurements around the whole figure. For precise measuring, plumb bobs were suspended from the perfectly level boom.

Miniature "pointing machines" were attached to the head of each model figure in Borglum's studio. The models' measurements were taken and multiplied by twelve to mark the corresponding "points" on the mountain. The first point would be the tip of the nose, since that was the most outstanding feature of the figure. From this mark, work would spread out to block the entire outline of the face. The accuracy of the measurements, together with the sculptor's careful eye for detail, kept the whole mountain project evolving in perspective.

Measurements were taken from the working models by using a system of booms and plumb bobs attached to the heads of each figure, shown here in Borglum's first studio.

Borglum himself studies the rock surface after wedging has prepared it for finishing work. Borglum's meticulous attention to detail and intimate knowledge of the chosen subjects brought to life the special character of each of the presidents.

Several hundred drill bits were sharpened daily by the blacksmith to accommodate the workers during periods of intense sculpting work.

Blacksmiths John Mikels, left, and Fred Robertson, right, inspect a bumper bit. These men, an important part of the carving operation, kept all the tools in repair and sharp for the day's work.

Bell
Photo
1937

Cable operators slowly unroll steel cables by hand, lowering workers over the mountainside. The transported workers sit on bosun's chairs or on small wooden platforms supported by the cables.

Sitting beneath the plaster model of Washington, a powderman prepares charges for use on one of the figures. Workmen blasted away most of the rock with dynamite, a practical necessity because of the enormous amount of stone that had to be removed.

Powermen Alfred Berg, left, and Spot Denton prepare dynamite charges, *1937.*

The plaster model of Lincoln's head hangs suspended under the hollowed mountain cheekbone so that a worker can directly transfer measurements with calipers from the cast to the rock wall. Casts of portions of the studio models were hoisted up and down the mountain to allow perfect precision in measuring the dimensions of the figures.

Blasting at the base of Washington's head in 1936.

Dynamite blasts away at President Lincoln's eye. Few photographs of the blasting exist.

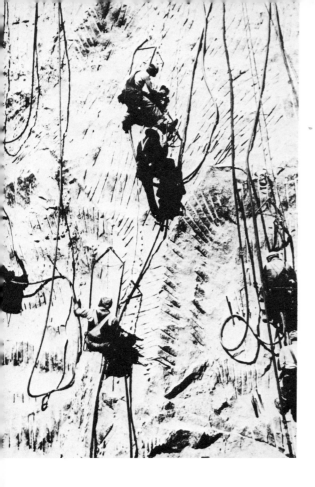

Workers block out a figure in preparation for the more detailed carving.

Using ladders and scaffolding, laborers drilled away at the granite mountain face for construction of Roosevelt's head in the late 1930s.

Suspended from a cable, a worker drills with a pneumatic tool. The workers were well paid during the lean years of the Depression. By the late 1930s drillers might earn 75 cents an hour, powdermen, $1.00, and carvers, $1.25.

After surface rock was removed, each figure was roughly blocked out. Workers used air-powered jackhammers to drill holes for the dynamite.

Workers began blocking out Abraham Lincoln's head in 1934.

William Tallman takes measurements by cable on the face of the mountain.

Safety precautions prevented any fatalities and reduced injuries in spite of the hazardous, dusty work.

Once the figures were blocked to within several inches, drill holes were shortened and more closely spaced. This "honeycombing" weakened the rock so that hand driven wedges could be used to pry off sections.

The Mount Rushmore Memorial in 1941.

Borglum examining the face of Lincoln.

Borglum thought it unwise to finish one head before starting another. He felt that a complete face might not fit artistically with the others, and he wanted to be free to blend all the figures into one sculptural unit toward the end of the project. From a bosun's chair Borglum (upper left) directs work on the Lincoln figure.

"Wedging," the removal of honey-combed rock, was the only sculpting process done by hand on Mount Rushmore.

Bell
Photo
1937

Workmen moved up and down the carving in portable crates as they refined Washington's head.

After holes were drilled in an area to be blasted, powdermen placed charges in them. Borglum used dynamite to remove the largest amount of rock from the monument.

As the mountain dictated the final design, money dictated its progress. When funds were plentiful, sometimes 70 men worked at a time; but when money grew scarce only one to four workers could be found scaling the cliffside. And there were many times of idleness on the mountain as Borglum frantically appealed for more funds. On the average though, 30 men worked the mountain through the years, year-round whenever possible. In extremely cold temperatures they worked from enclosed cages lowered over the top.

With an eye sensititive to the effects of light and shadow on the figures, Borglum experimented with shifting the alignment of each figure in his studio. He turned Washington's head about 20 degrees further south to take advantage of the lighting. It was this genius and care that today brings alive the eyes of the presidents, even capturing the delicacy of Roosevelt's spectacles.

For the most perfect accuracy possible, the workers hauled five-foot models of each head up the mountain in order to use them as guides for the "points" by transferring the measurements directly. Mountain carving, however, was not an exact science and the work had to be studied and changed each day. Borglum felt that the piece must work as a whole, and that each figure had to interact with the others, so he conducted work on them simultaneously throughout the entire construction.

Once dynamite had blasted out the surface for each figure, the work was pursued by hand. Creating a honeycomb effect, the workers drilled holes

The measuring boom (pointing machine) used to mark off details of the face, rests on top of George Washington's head. Cables hold the laborers working from wooden cages.

into the rock every two or three inches. They drove steel wedges into the holes to pry off the rock to the desired surface. The final stage of carving employed a "bumping" process devised for the project. Workers smoothed the granite with small air guns that used four-cornered facing bits. One can see the results of this finish work on the rock today. Scaffolding built from heavy bridge timbers, bolted into the rock, supported the finish crews. The strong wooden network held firm even through the blustery mountain winters.

Extreme caution was the word during the dynamite process; it was vital not to blast away more rock than needed. The slow process was further hampered by money problems which delayed construction much longer than Borglum had envisioned. In fact, he had designed the models down to their waists, but the actual carving was never to evolve that far.

Carved to the scale of a 465-foot-tall person, the measurements of the mountain are truly astounding. The height above the base is 500 feet; the height of the figures, 60 feet; each nose is about 20 feet high; each mouth, 18 feet wide; and the eyes are 11 feet across. The mountain itself rises 5,725 feet above sea level.

How long will the mountain of presidents survive? The granite weathers slowly and the Park Service maintains the sculpture with annual care and upkeep. Odds are that people thousands of years from now will stand at the base and marvel at the magnificent monument to America that Gutzon Borglum engineered.

Measurements made on the model were multiplied by 12 and transferred to the mountain by use of similar—but much larger—devices mounted on the sculptured heads.

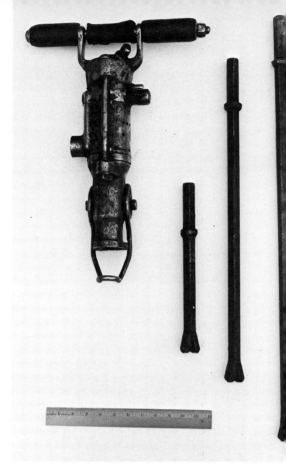

To drill holes for explosives, laborers employed First Stage tools: a jack-hammer and 4-star drill bits.

Edging cleavage lines for explosives required these Second Stage tools. From the left is a Sullivian plug drill, a point, a channel iron and a point and hammer.

A Dallet hand facer and bumping bits bumped and smoothed the rock in the final stage of construction.

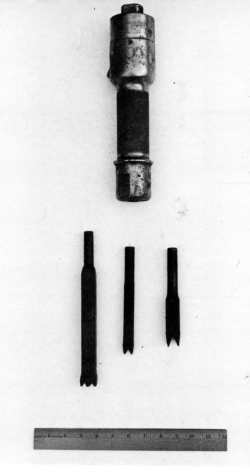

These Third Stage tools were used for honeycombing/wedging of the rock. On the left are 4-star drill bits, in the center a Sullivian plug drill, and on the right a mallet and wedge for removing the honeycombed rock.

MOUNT RUSHMORE
National Memorial
THE SHRINE OF DEMOCRACY

Borglum produced these bro-chures during the construc-tion years to try to promote interest and raise money for the memorial.

CHAPTER FIVE

Final Years

The increased progress of the final years was often overshadowed by financial crises and bitter controversy between Borglum, the Park Service and the Mount Rushmore Commission. The design to complete the total upper bodies of the figures had to be abandoned; only Washington had his neck and part of his lapel finished. By the latter years the last figure, President Theodore Roosevelt, was taking shape, and the other figures were well defined.

Borglum had spent some of his own money and donated much time to the project without adequate compensation. He was having an increasingly hard time wringing funds from the federal coffers for a decent contract to continue work. In 1937 he made every effort to get a renewed contract with an increase in his honorarium, but the federal government turned a deaf ear. He did not receive any pay for that year until 1938.

The conflicts with the federal agencies abated when President Franklin D. Roosevelt appointed a new Mount Rushmore Commission in 1938 and placed the financial responsibilities under the Treasury Department. To Borglum's relief, the memorial was no longer under the National Park Service's jurisdiction.

The following year, Congress approved an appropriation of $300,000 to finish work. On July 2, 1939, the figure of Roosevelt was unveiled. Borglum had a new, larger studio built, and threw himself into the Hall of Records project.

In another reversal, however, the federal government reorganized itself, returning the memorial to the administration of the Park Service. This was a serious setback for Borglum because the new policy forced him to abandon the Hall of Records project and concentrate solely on finishing the four figures on the face of Rushmore. By this time, his son, Lincoln, had taken over most of the construction and administrative duties on the site.

As a new decade approached, the Mount Rushmore spectacle drew more and more visitors. The sculpture was nearing completion and the Park Service had upgraded the tourist facilities, making the monument one of the most important landmarks in the nation.

Almost 74 years old, Borglum had dedicated the past sixteen years to his unsurpassed work of art, either on the mountain or on the road raising money. In spite of the obstacles and countless delays, Borglum never gave up; he set out for the midwest in January 1941, on a fundraising tour—it was to be his last journey. He never made it back to see his beloved mountain.

Built in 1928, Borglum's first studio faces Mount Rushmore. All that remains today are the fireplaces just below the Visitor Center. The sculptor moved to his second studio in 1939.

Borglum's second studio, built in 1939, served as a visitor center until completion of the present center in 1964. The studio, now a museum, houses the original Rushmore and Hall of Records plaster models.

The rakish Borglum sports a scarf as he poses with the Second Mount Rushmore National Memorial Commission in August 1939, on the steps of his studio.

"Pointers" James LaRue on the left and Matt Reilly on the right talk with Lincoln Borglum, center, on the mountain. "Pointers" measured the plaster models and located the corresponding points on the mountain. Reilly also made plaster casts of some parts of the original plaster model used on the mountain for detail work.

Borglum not only loved but needed all the publicity he could get to keep his project before the public. Radio station KOA, Denver is shown here in the late 1930s conducting an interview. Borglum poses second from the right.

Borglum describes the details of his monumental sculpture to South Dakota Governor Tom Berry and President Franklin D. Roosevelt, who journeyed to the Black Hills for the dedication of the Jefferson figure on August 30, 1936.

Portable scaffolding and sheds--for protection from the weather--were moved as work progressed on the sculpture. Taken in 1938 or 1939, this photo illustrates work on Roosevelt's head.

Scaffolding honeycombs the head of Theodore Roosevelt in May 1939, when three of the four figures were complete or nearly complete. Roosevelt was the last figure finished.

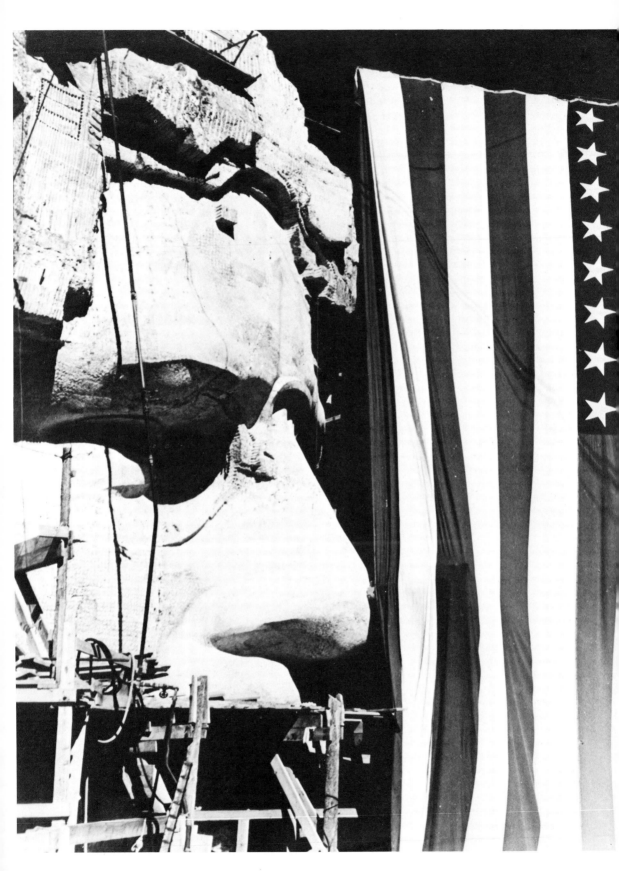

A partially complete Roosevelt noses into the Stars and Stripes.

A plaster model of George Washington lies crated in a wooden frame for the move to Borglum's new studio. The viewing scope in the background attests to the popularity of the project even before completion.

Workmen move the plaster model of Mount Rushmore in parts from Borglum's old studio to the new one. The model had to be cut into four pieces, fitted into a wooden crate and carefully lowered down the stairs.

A spidery web of catwalks and cables surrounds the Mount Rushmore National Monument in 1941, as work nears completion. Workmen used buildings atop the sculpture to store machinery and equipment as well as for workshops. The laborers slept in bunkhouses at the base of the mountain.

The mountain crew poses before the nearly completed memorial in 1941. Front row, left to right: Jay Shepard, winchman; Alton Leach, assistant carver; Clyde Denton, chief powderman; Pat Bintuff, assistant carver; Bill Reynolds, senior driller; Bay Jurisch, toolman; Jim LaRue, carver; Frank Maxwell, assistant carver and John Raga, mason. Back row, left to right: Orwell Peterson, laborer; Ernest Raga, assistant carver; Red Anderson, carver; Matt Reilly, chief pointer; Ray Grover, winchman; Hap Anderson, carver; Joe Brunner, carver; Ed Hayes, hoist operator; Marion Watson, carver; Gus Schram, assistant carver; Earl Oaks, senior driller; Bob Heinbaugh, senior driller; Basil Canfield, compressor engineer; Bob Christon, blacksmith and the sculptor's son, Lincoln Borglum, superintendent.

THE FINAL ACT

When Gutzon Borglum died in Chicago, Illinois, on March 6, 1941, many of his admirers wanted to entomb his body at the Mount Rushmore site, but his family interceded, and, honoring his wishes, arranged to have him buried in California. After three and a half years of complications, his body was finally laid to rest in the Forest Lawn Memorial Park, Glendale, California.

Insistent on not detracting from the presidential monument, Borglum would not even allow his name to appear any place on the mountain.

After Borglum's death, the Mount Rushmore National Memorial Commission asked his son, Lincoln, to continue on as superintendent of the park and to work on the carvings. However, national defense was taking ever more funds out of the national budget in the early 1940s, and appropriations for the monument were drastically reduced.

Lincoln worked in refining the heads of President Roosevelt and Lincoln. He blocked out Jefferson's collar and finished Washington's coat collar and lapels before funds were exhausted in the fall of 1941. Work stopped on October 31, but Lincoln Borglum stayed on as superintendent of the site until 1944.

The Hall of Records and stairway project remains on the drawing board; no work has been done since 1941 on the exterior or interior of the mountain.

Anticipating shifts in the rock structure, Gutzon Borglum created a special mixture for patching cracks. A Park Service crew uses this same mixture to fill occasional rifts in the rock sculpture on its annual inspection of the monument's surface. No major splits have been detected in the rock to date.

The total expenditure on Borglum's tribute to America amounted to over $989,000; the federal government contributed $836,000, private sources, the remainder. The National Park Service has made vast improvements in the visitor accommodations at the site, and today Mount Rushmore is one of the most heavily visited attractions in the National Park system. Gutzon Borglum would smile proudly to know that the many years he dedicated to his unique American masterpiece has given millions of people pleasure from all over the world.

G utzon Borglum's most ambitious dream, a Hall of Records hollowed out of the mountain itself, has yet to be realized. His plans for the interior of Mount Rushmore equaled the magnitude of the presidential sculpture on its exterior. In a passionate speech to President Franklin D. Roosevelt, who was on hand for the unveiling of the head of Jefferson in August 1936, Borglum proposed his phenomenal scheme:

> *There should be a great stairway of stone cut from the local rock on the east facade, easy to ascend and, back of the sculpture into the mountain itself—a great room, at least 90 by 110 feet should be cut. Into this room the records of what our people aspired to and what they have accomplished should be collected and preserved and on the walls of this room should be cut the literal record of the conception of our republic; its successful creation; the record of its westward movement to the Pacific; its presidents; how the Memorial was built and, frankly, why. I have prepared the design for these.*

His idea was not only to inscribe on the walls of the Hall the great documents of American history, but to place within statues of prominent American historical figures. He even proposed to carve the history of the United States in four languages—English, Latin, Greek and Sanskrit.

The Hall of Records design had haunted Borglum for years. References to different versions of it appear in speeches and correspondence in the late 1920s and early '30s. He had toyed with the idea for a great hall during his work on the Confederate monument at Stone Mountain, Georgia, but he left the project before any concrete plans were formed.

The dimensions of his proposal for Mount Rushmore more than a decade later were staggering: the Hall would be two-thirds of the way up the mountain, its entrance cut through a small gorge across the ravine and to the right of the presidential heads; pylons cut into the granite, 140 feet high, would flank the 20-foot-high, 12-foot-wide entrance; the floor of the Hall would be 100 feet by 80 feet, with a 32-foot-high ceiling; and, finally, bronze and glass cabinets would hold the records of America history inside the Hall.

Borglum designed a great stone stairway to be built from his studio to the Hall's entrance. The steps would be 15-20 feet wide and 18 inches deep. Senator Norbeck pushed for the Civilian Conservation Corps to build the stairway, but so intent was Borglum on having complete artistic control that he even offered to pay for the stairway himself—in spite of meager funds—in order to build it himself.

An old friend of Borglum's and his official photographer, Charles D'Emery visited the memorial in the summer of 1937. The concept of the great Hall so impressed him that he wrote:

Directly in back of the mountaintop is a deep gully about forty feet wide, lined on each side by a solid wall of granite a hundred feet high. Into one of these walls Mr. Borglum intends to cut a huge chamber which will be used to store the archives of our early American history. This room, being an integral part of the mountain itself, will be imperishable and preserve for untold generations to come, the history of our country when the present civilization has been dust for a thousand centuries.

Borglum even contacted the famous architect, Frank Lloyd Wright, who agreed to work on the project with him. For the entire Hall of Records and staircase project, Borglum estimated that construction costs would approximate $197,000. The Second Mount Rushmore National Memorial Commission, created on July 1, 1938, gave the sculptor much more financial latitude in finishing the memorial than the First Commission had; with the large appropriation of $300,000, Borglum immediately started to carve the Hall of Records in the summer of '38.

But the extraordinary Hall of history was destined never to be finished. Pressing national defense needs usurped the appropriated funds. When the Park Service took over administration of the monument on July 1, 1939, the decision was made to complete the four faces on the mountain's exterior before work continued on the Hall.

Today, the entrance penetrates 70 feet into the mountain. Talk of finishing Borglum's dream remains only talk. Perhaps one day the Hall will become a reality, the rubble at the base of the mountain removed, and additional work done on the four figures. It will take a determined visionary as strong as Gutzon Borglum to pursue that goal.

Arched like a Roman aqueduct, a great stairway was to ascend from Borglum's studio to the entrance of the Hall of Records, as seen in his drawing.

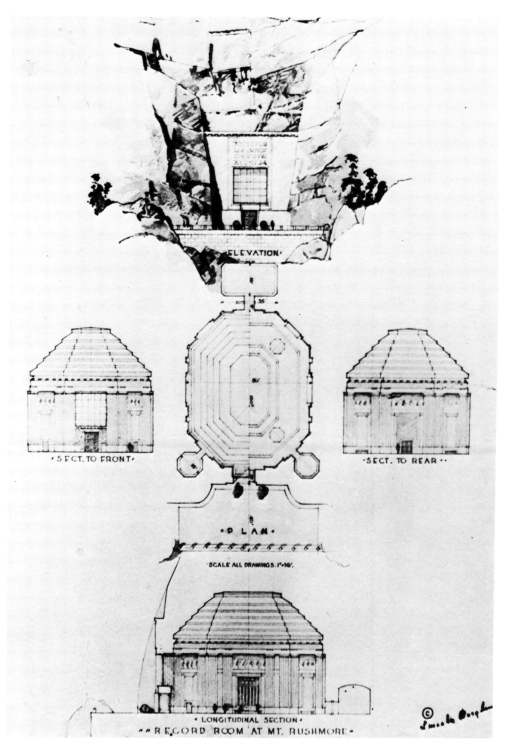

Borglum planned an octagonal Hall of Records that would be hollowed out of the heart of Mount Rushmore. He envisioned an impregnable mountain fortress that would house the entire history of the United States in bronze and glass cabinets, but the nation's preparations for defense absorbed the funds necessary for the project, which is still on the drawing board.

Workmen carve the massive entrance for the never-to-be-finished Hall of Records, Borglum's dream plan for preserving American history. Today it stands partially carved in the valley directly behind the presidential heads.

The partially completed entrance stands as a reminder of one of Borglum's great dreams.

Borglum penetrated about 70 feet into the mountain before he was forced to abandon the Hall project. This recent photograph shows how the interior looks today.

Borglum sculpted plaster models of the unfinished Hall of Records. The large model has a scale of 1" = 2' and is on display in the studio museum.

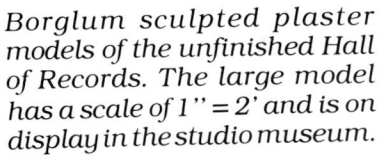

CHAPTER SEVEN

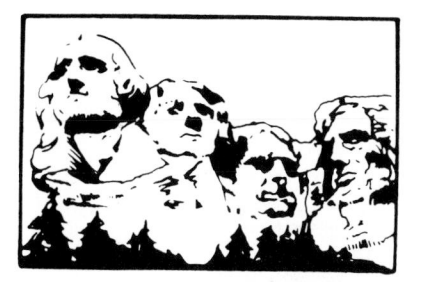

Modern Views

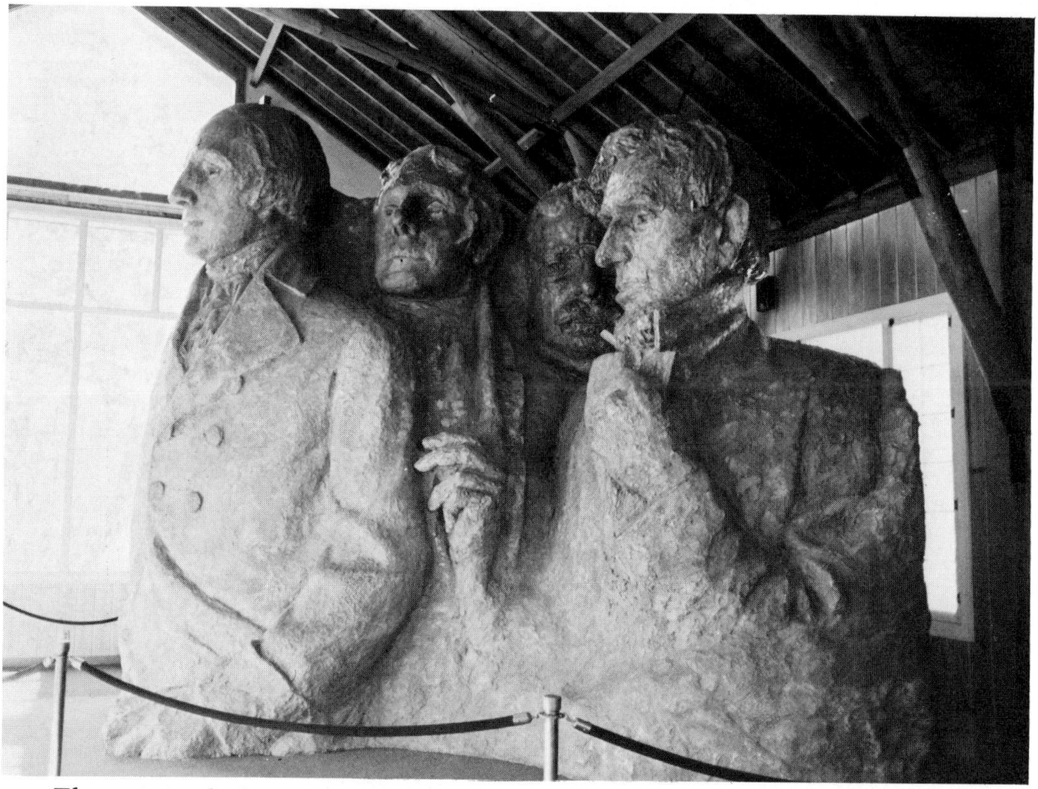

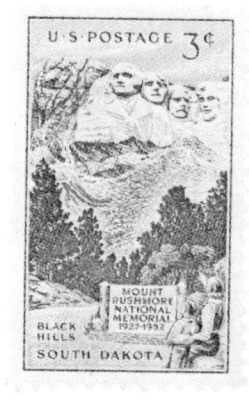

The original plaster cast of the proposed memorial, now located in the second studio (museum), was used by Borglum to transfer measurements to the mountain itself.

This commemorative stamp was issued in 1952 to honor the 25th anniversary of the Mount Rushmore Memorial.

George Washington was the first of the four figures to be carved on Mount Rushmore. Sculptor Borglum decided Washington should hold the leading and dominant position in the carving because of his contributions toward our country's independence, constitution and liberty.

Patron of the Lewis and Clark expedition to the Pacific and champion of agrarian democracy, Thomas Jefferson wrote the Declaration of Independence. Borglum reveals the refined, inventive spirit of the Virginia statesman, whose forwarding of the principle of self-government insured that the nation would be governed by the people.

The eyeglasses that bridge Theodore Roosevelt's nose attest to the inspired attention to detail of Borglum. Of the four presidents on Mount Rushmore, Roosevelt was the most recent, a man who was president in our own century. Gutzon Borglum knew Roosevelt personally. Roosevelt's robust character, vigor and ability to think big typified to Borglum the character and thought of Americanism.

Borglum captures the depth of sadness in the face of Abraham Lincoln, a president who braved the arduous task of preserving the Union through its bloodiest war. Borglum respected Lincoln's steadfast convictions and named his son after him.

View of the completed Mount Rushmore National Memorial (showing Washington, Jefferson, T. Roosevelt and Lincoln).

Like a fly on his nose, a Park Service employee makes a routine inspection of Lincoln's face. A crew inspects the entire sculpture each year to ensure that succeeding generations will see the monument as Borglum intended.

The shaft of granite protruding from the hollowed area of Lincoln's eyes catches the light and gives them a life-like twinkle. Shadows cast by the natural light from above create remarkable contrasts of light and dark. Visitors to Mount Rushmore are often amazed at the living character that seems to shine from the eyes of the presidents.

Two-man hand winches hauled men, equipment and tools up and down the mountain face. Strapped in bosun's chairs as in the past, today's Park Service maintenance crews use the same equipment on their annual inspection of the sculpture.

After the monument's figures were roughed in by blasting, these Final Stage tools were employed by Borglum to perfect the sculptures.

SCULPTOR'S TOOL

A rock drill on display in the museum area.

One of the three compressors that provided power to the pneumatic tools is now preserved by the Park Service. It is now housed inside a shed below the studio museum.

The two original fireplaces are all that remain from the first studio.

A bust of Gutzon Borglum, sculptor of Mount Rushmore, stands in front of the site of his first studio, just below the Visitor Center.

Ed Hayes, a former tram operator on the mountain (1936-1941) talks to visitors on the Visitor Center terrace in the summer of 1982.

Borglum's second studio, now a museum for the memorial, ranges beneath the sculptor's tribute to America.

In 1959, MGM Studios filmed portions of Alfred Hitchcock's North By Northwest at the memorial. It starred Cary Grant, Eva Marie Saint, James Mason, Leo G. Carroll and Martin Landau. Saint, Grant and Mason pose for tourists at the base of the monument to advertise the newly released film.
Academy of Motion Picture Arts and Sciences

The climax of the film, North by Northwest, shows Cary Grant and Eva Marie Saint being chased by two villains between the president's faces on Mount Rushmore. These scenes were actually filmed on mock-up faces in Hollywood. MGM had previously agreed with the Park Service that no scenes of violence would be filmed near the heads. The Park Service received complaints of the desecration of the memorial from this scene and MGM was asked to drop the credit line for the Park Service from the movie's introduction.
Academy of Motion Picture Arts and Sciences

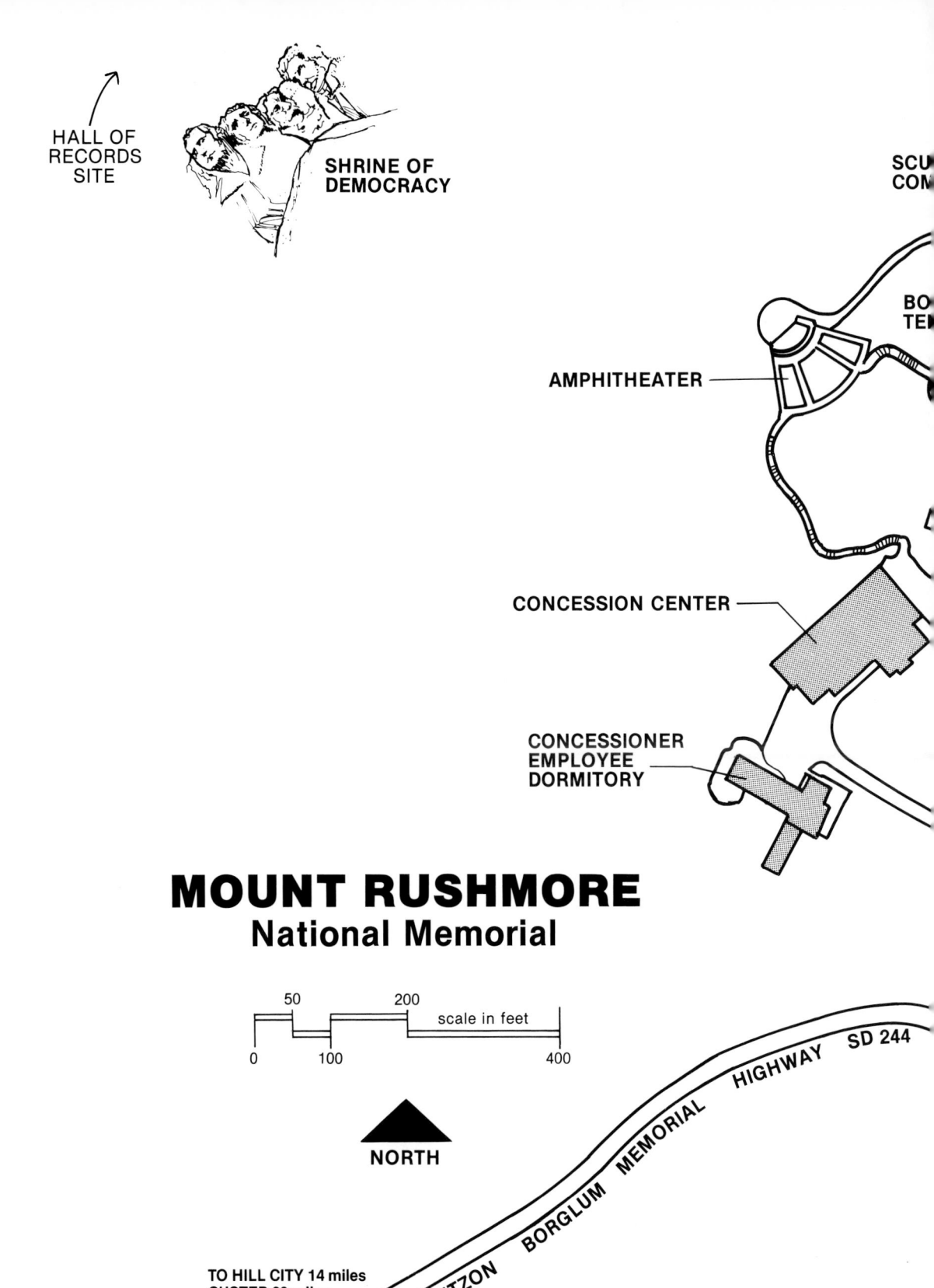

HALL OF
RECORDS
SITE

SHRINE OF
DEMOCRACY

SCU
COM

BO
TE

AMPHITHEATER

CONCESSION CENTER

CONCESSIONER
EMPLOYEE
DORMITORY

MOUNT RUSHMORE
National Memorial

50   200
scale in feet

0   100   400

NORTH

GUTZON BORGLUM MEMORIAL HIGHWAY SD 244

TO HILL CITY 14 miles
CUSTER 20 miles

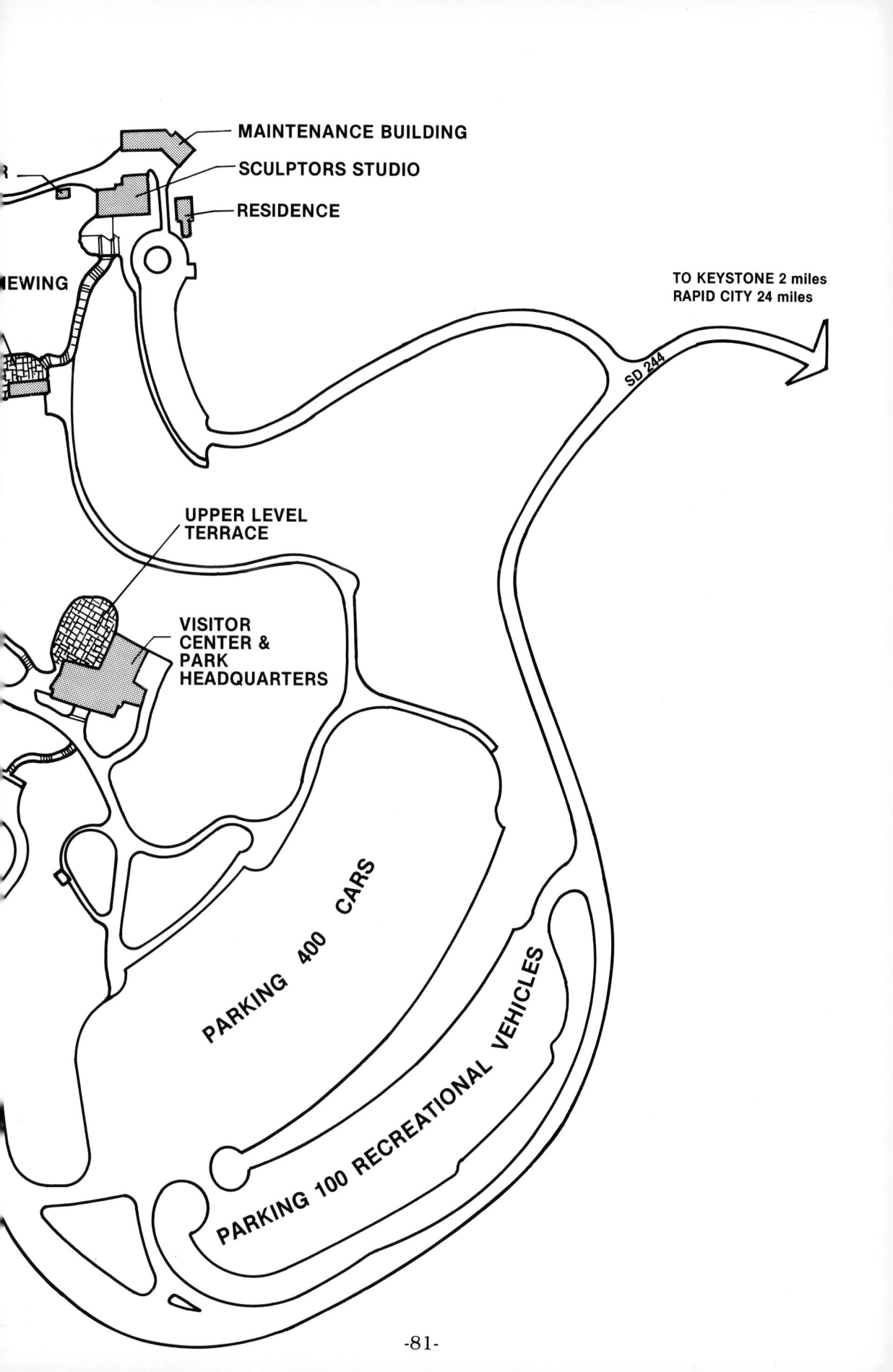

MAINTENANCE BUILDING

SCULPTORS STUDIO

RESIDENCE

R

EWING

TO KEYSTONE 2 miles
RAPID CITY 24 miles

SD 244

UPPER LEVEL
TERRACE

VISITOR
CENTER &
PARK
HEADQUARTERS

PARKING 400 CARS

PARKING 100 RECREATIONAL VEHICLES

Bibliography

Casey, Robert and Mary Borglum, *Give the Man Room,* the Story of Gutzon Borglum, the Bobbs-Merrill Co., 1952.

Dean, Robert J., *Living Granite,* the Story of Borglum and the Mount Rushmore Memorial, Viking Press, 1949.

Fite, Gilbert C., *Mount Rushmore,* University of Oklahoma Press, 1952.

Price, Willadene, *Gutzon Borglum, the Man Who Carved a Mountain,* 1961.

Zeitner, June Culp and Lincoln Borglum, *Borglum's Unfinished Dream,* Mount Rushmore, North Plains Press, Box 1830, Aberdeen, S.D., 1976.

About the Author

Stan Cohen resides in Missoula, Montana, with his wife, Anne, and two sons. He has a degree in geology from West Virginia University and was engaged in several businesses before starting his publishing career in 1976. To date he has authored or co-authored 18 books and published a total of 30 pictorial history books. He has been fascinated with Mount Rushmore since first visiting the site more than 23 years ago.